Yosemite
National Park

by Mike Graf

Reading Consultant:
Dr. Robert Miller
Professor of Special Education
Minnesota State University, Mankato

Bridgestone Books

an imprint of Capstone Press

M .   a

Bridgestone Books are published by Capstone Press
151 Good Counsel Drive, P.O. Box 669, Mankato, Minnesota 56002
http://www.capstone-press.com

Library of Congress Cataloging-in-Publication Data
Graf, Mike.
   Yosemite National Park / by Mike Graf.
   v. cm.—(National parks)
   Includes bibliographical references and index.
   Contents: Yosemite National Park—How Yosemite formed—People in Yosemite—
Animals—Plants—Weather—Activities—Safety—Park issues—Map activity—About
national parks—Words to know—Read more—Useful addresses—Internet sites.
   ISBN 0-7368-1380-2 (hardcover)
   1. Yosemite National Park (Calif.)—Juvenile literature. [1. Yosemite National Park (Calif.)
2. National parks and reserves.] I. Title. II. National parks (Mankato, Minn.)
F868.Y6 G73 2003
917.94'470454—dc21
                                                                    2001008097

Editorial Credits
Blake A. Hoena, editor; Karen Risch, product planning editor; Linda Clavel, designer; Anne
   McMullen, illustrator; Alta Schaffer, photo researcher

Photo Credits
Beth Davidow, 4, 6
Digital Stock, cover
Digital Vision, 1
Doranne Jacobson, 8
Eda Rogers, 16
Ernest H. Rogers, 12 (right)
Joe McDonald, 10, 18
Jon Gnass/Gnass Photo Images, 14
Neil Montanus/Houserstock, 12 (left), 17

1 2 3 4 5 6 07 06 05 04 03 02

Table of Contents

Yosemite National Park. 5
How Yosemite Formed 7
People in Yosemite 9
Animals 11
Plants 13
Weather 15
Activities 16
Safety 17
Park Issues 19
Map Activity 21
About National Parks 22
Words to Know 23
Read More 23
Useful Addresses. 24
Internet Sites 24
Index 24

California

Yosemite National Park

In 1864, President Abraham Lincoln signed a bill to protect Yosemite Valley. This law was the first of its kind. Never before had the U.S. government set aside scenic land just for people's enjoyment.

In 1872, the U.S. government set aside land for the first national park. National parks are created to protect unique natural areas. People cannot hunt or build on national park lands. But they can camp, hike, and view wildlife in these parks. Yosemite became a national park in 1890.

Yosemite National Park is located in central California. The park is within the Sierra Nevada Mountains. Yosemite covers almost 1,200 square miles (3,100 square kilometers) of land.

One of the most interesting features of the park is Yosemite Valley. This valley is 7 miles (11 kilometers) long and 1 mile (1.6 kilometers) wide. It contains steep cliffs, granite peaks, and waterfalls.

Yosemite Falls is found in Yosemite Valley.

How Yosemite Formed

Many mountains in the Sierra Nevada Mountains are made of granite. This hard rock formed in the area about 100 million years ago. Magma, or melted rock, flowed upward from Earth's center toward its surface. As the magma cooled, it formed into granite.

Most of the granite formed under Earth's surface. But over millions of years, erosion uncovered the granite. Flowing water from streams and rivers washed away soil covering the rock. The Sierra Nevada Mountains formed as more and more soil washed away.

Glaciers also helped shape the Yosemite area. Glaciers dug out much of Yosemite Valley. These slow-moving sheets of ice smoothed the mountains' granite surfaces. Glaciers also pushed up rocks and dirt into moraines. Moraines are piles of rock and dirt that form natural dams and create lakes.

Many interesting features can be found in Yosemite Valley such as El Capitan's steep cliff face (left).

People in Yosemite

Ahwahneechee Indians of the Miwok tribe lived in Yosemite for more than 7,000 years. Their arrowheads and grinding rocks have been found throughout the park.

In 1848, the California gold rush began. Gold was found in the Sierra Nevada's foothills. Many people rushed to the area with hopes of finding gold and becoming rich. American Indians in the area fought to protect their lands from these people.

James Savage led the Mariposa Battalion. This group of soldiers helped protect miners from American Indian attacks. While searching for Indians, Savage's men came upon Yosemite Valley. The valley's scenery amazed the men and they told others about it.

By the 1860s, the U.S. government passed laws to protect the area. These laws protected Yosemite Valley and the Mariposa Grove of sequoias. This group of large trees is part of Yosemite National Park.

This photograph shows a rebuilt Miwok home in Yosemite National Park.

10

Animals

Many animals live throughout Yosemite National Park. Skunks, porcupines, and mule deer live in Yosemite's foothills. Steller's jays, scrub jays, wrens, and hawks also live in this area.

Predators such as coyotes, bobcats, and ringtails live in the park's forests. These animals hunt other park animals for food. Owls fly through Yosemite's forests looking for prey. Predators such as mountain lions hunt in the mountains.

Several other animals also live in the park's mountains. Bighorn sheep are able to climb steep, rocky mountain slopes. Marmots live high in the mountains. These squirrel-like animals often are seen lying in the sun. Fish such as trout swim in mountain streams. Black bears roam throughout the mountains.

Steller's jays live throughout much of Yosemite National Park.

Grizzly Giant (right) is the fifth largest tree in the world. This sequoia stands more than 200 feet (60 meters) tall and is more than 2,700 years old. Below, a man stands next to a sequoia in the Mariposa Grove.

12

Plants

Sequoias once grew in many places throughout North America. But now they grow only on the western side of the Sierra Nevada Mountains. These trees are considered the largest and some of the oldest living things in the world. The oldest sequoia is almost 3,000 years old.

In Yosemite's foothills, forests of gray pine and oak trees grow. Forests of ponderosa pine, sugar pine, cedar, fir, oak, and dogwood trees grow around Yosemite Valley.

In the mountains, forests of Jeffrey pine, fir, white pine, and aspen trees grow. Lodgepole pines also are common in the mountains. American Indians used these tall, straight trees to build their homes.

In Yosemite's high mountains, few trees can grow because of the harsh weather. But many wildflowers grow in this area. Lichen and mosses also grow high in the mountains.

Weather

Spanish explorers named the mountain range that surrounds Yosemite National Park. "Sierra Nevada" means "snowy range" in Spanish. In winter, up to 5 feet (1.5 meters) of snow can fall during one storm. Most of Yosemite's precipitation falls between December and April.

The snow begins to melt in the spring. Water from melting snow swells Yosemite's mountain streams and rivers. The park's waterfalls are their fullest at this time of year.

Summers in Yosemite are warm and dry. The temperature can even reach 100 degrees Fahrenheit (38 degrees Celsius) in Yosemite Valley. Temperatures get cooler higher up in the mountains. Yosemite's waterfalls start to dry up in summer.

Fall usually is dry. The nights begin to get cooler. Many of Yosemite's trees turn colors in October and November. By November or early December, the first snow falls.

Summer days in Yosemite can be warm and sunny.

Activities

Many people enjoy rock climbing in Yosemite. The park has small cliffs for beginners to climb. More experienced climbers may attempt to climb El Capitan or Half Dome. These climbs can last for days. The park also has a rock climbing school. They even offer classes for children.

Almost everyone hikes when they come to Yosemite. People can hike to waterfalls, giant trees, and other scenic areas. Visitors also can camp overnight in the park.

Safety

Hikers and climbers must be careful in the park. The park has many steep, rocky hiking trails. Many of the park's tall peaks are difficult to climb. Rock climbers need to bring the proper equipment with them on climbs.

In spring and early summer, Yosemite's rivers, streams, and waterfalls are at their fullest. Visitors need to be careful near these waterways. Rushing water can quickly carry a person downstream.

Park Issues

In the early 1900s, black bears were breaking into nearby restaurants in search of food. Park workers began to lead the bears to food at garbage dumps in the area. Watching the bears feed at the dumps became a popular attraction for park visitors. But this activity also caused problems. Some people were injured as they tried to feed the bears. Over time, the dumps were all closed.

Bears are wild animals. But they can lose their fear of people when fed by people. They then may walk into campsites or break into cars in search of food. They may even become aggressive toward park visitors. Bears that threaten visitors may have to be killed to prevent people from being injured.

Today, park workers are teaching people how to help keep bears wild. The park also has laws against feeding bears. Park visitors must store their food in bear-proof food lockers. Bears cannot get at the food in these containers.

Black bears live in Yosemite National Park.

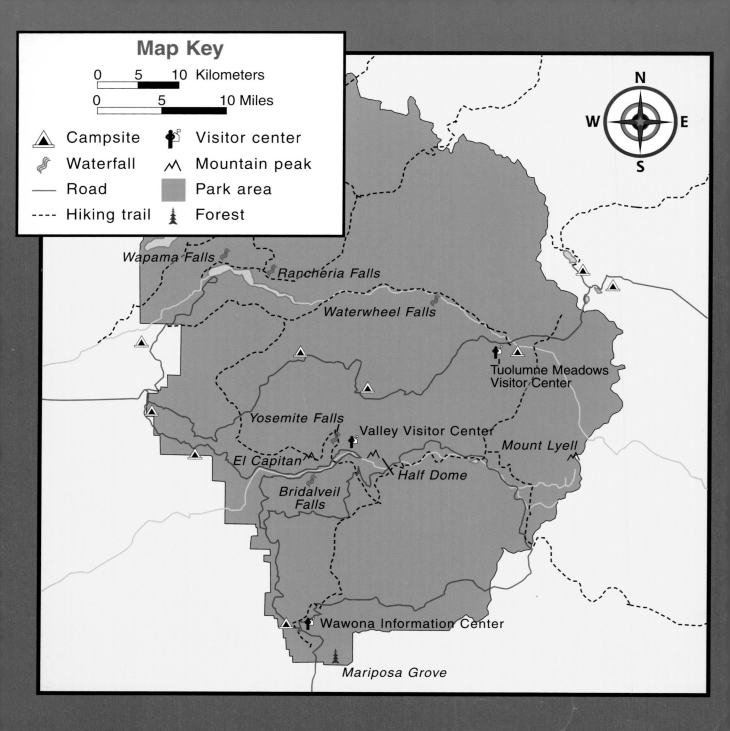

Map Key

0   5   10   Kilometers

0   5   10   Miles

△ Campsite   👤 Visitor center
🌊 Waterfall   ⋀ Mountain peak
— Road   ▨ Park area
---- Hiking trail   🌲 Forest

Wapama Falls
Rancheria Falls
Waterwheel Falls

Tuolumne Meadows
Visitor Center

Yosemite Falls

Valley Visitor Center

Mount Lyell

El Capitan

Half Dome

Bridalveil
Falls

Wawona Information Center

Mariposa Grove

N
W   E
S

Map Activity

Maps have many symbols on them. These symbols help you learn what you can find in the map's area. Park maps show sites you can visit, hiking trails, and other features within the park. Learn to use the map's key to understand what is on the map.

What You Need
Ruler

What You Do
1. While visiting a national park, it is a good idea to find out information about the park. Visitor centers will provide this information. Can you find one on the map?
2. There are several campsites for people to stay overnight in Yosemite National Park. Find the symbol for a campsite in the map's key. Then locate a campsite on the map. What visitor center is closest to your campsite? You can use your ruler to measure the distance.
3. People hike to see many of the waterfalls within the park. Look for the symbol of a waterfall in the map's key. How many waterfalls can you find on the map? Do you need to use roads, hiking trails, or both to get to the waterfalls?

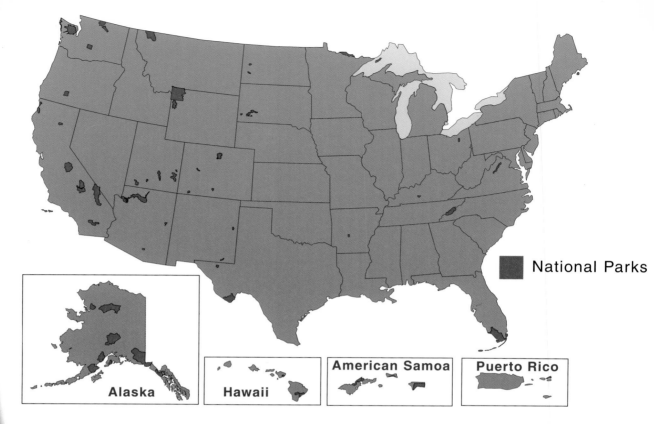

National Parks

Alaska

Hawaii

American Samoa

Puerto Rico

About National Parks

In 1872, the U.S. government set aside land for Yellowstone
National Park. This park was the first national park in the
world. The government sets up national parks to protect
natural areas such as Yellowstone and Yosemite. These parks
allow people to enjoy park lands. People can camp, hike, and
view the scenery in these areas. But they cannot hunt or
build on park lands. Today, there are more than 50 national
parks in the United States.

Words to Know

erosion (ee-ROH-zhuhn)—the wearing away of land by water or wind

foothill (FUT-hil)—a low hill at the base of a mountain

glacier (GLAY-shur)—a slow-moving sheet of ice found on mountains and in polar regions

harsh (HARSH)—unpleasant or hard

lichen (LYE-ken)—a mosslike growth on rocks and trees

magma (MAG-muh)—melted rock that is found beneath Earth's crust

precipitation (pri-sip-i-TAY-shuhn)—the rain and snow an area receives

predator (PRED-uh-tur)—an animal that hunts other animals for food

scenic (SEE-nik)—a place that has beautiful natural surroundings

unique (yoo-NEEK)—one of a kind

Read More

Halvorsen, Lisa. *Yosemite.* Letters Home from National Parks. Woodbridge, Conn.: Blackbirch Press, 2000.

Petersen, David. *National Parks.* A True Book. New York: Children's Press, 2001.

Raatma, Lucia. *Our National Parks.* Let's See. Minneapolis: Compass Point Books, 2002.

Useful Addresses

National Park Service
1849 C Street NW
Washington, DC 20240

Yosemite National Park
Superintendent
P.O. Box 577
Yosemite National Park,
  CA 95389

Internet Sites

National Park Service—Yosemite National Park
http://www.nps.gov/yose
U.S. National Parks Net—Yosemite National Park
http://www.yosemite.national-park.com
Yosemite National Park
http://www.yosemitepark.com

Index

American Indians, 9, 13
animals, 5, 11, 19
bears, 11, 19
glaciers, 7
hiking, 5, 16, 17
magma, 7
plants, 11, 13, 15, 16
rock climbing, 16, 17

safety, 17, 19
Savage, James, 9
sequoias, 9, 12, 13
Sierra Nevada Mountains, 5,
    7, 9, 13, 15
waterfalls, 5, 15, 16, 17
weather, 13, 15
Yosemite Valley, 5, 7, 9, 13, 15

11/06 12   10/06